THE MISSING LINK

Sanjay Koul 'Arigam'

Qurate
quratebooks.com

The Mising Link
Sanjay Koul 'Arigam'

Published in 2025

© Published by

Qurate Books Pvt. Ltd.
Goa 403523, India
www.quratebooks.com
Tel: 1800-210-6527, Email: info@quratebooks.com

ISBN: 978-93-58983-31-9

PROLOGUE

4:32 AM | Monday

The alarm doesn't wake me anymore. My body knows the drill.

It is still dark outside. Pune is quiet, almost unwilling to let go of the night. I pack my bag silently, careful not to wake my son. I glance at the clock — I have 18 minutes before I leave. Enough time for a cup of coffee, but not enough for a real goodbye.

The engine starts quietly. I reverse my car out of the ground-floor parking, into a morning that hasn't yet begun. My wife waves from the balcony - half-asleep, yet fully present. It is our unsaid ritual now. A wave, a nod, a promise to return Friday night. Always Friday night.

The engine hums as I head toward the express way. Another week begins. Another five days in Mumbai, sometimes even six.

For some, it is a commute. For me, it is a recalibration - of roles, responsibilities, and emotions. I am not just traveling 160 kilometers; I am shifting between two versions of myself. The father who leaves Pune. The professional who arrives in Mumbai.

And every single time I cross the familiar bends of the Mumbai–Pune Express way, I see it - the massive tunnels disappearing underground, part of an under-construction project suspended like a thought half-finished. They call it 'The Missing Link' - a project meant to make the journey smoother, faster, better. Promised for years. Still incomplete.

Just like me.

This book is not about traffic jams or job titles. It is about the space between decisions and consequences, between ambition and absence, between Pune and Mumbai, ... and the quiet discoveries made on the road that connects them.

This is my story. And perhaps, a little bit of yours too.

INTRODUCTION

The Missing Link

There is a road I have travelled more than hundreds of times in the last three years.

Not just a physical stretch between Pune and Mumbai - but a deeper, often quieter road that runs through decisions, distances, and dreams.

In 2022, I made what many would call a bold career move: I left the comfort and predictability of a settled job for years to join a new company based in Mumbai. On the surface, it was a professional switch. In reality, it turned out to be a personal transformation.

That decision set the stage for a life in transit — Pune on weekends, Mumbai on weekdays. The week began before dawn every Monday and ended late Friday nights. It was a rhythm that demanded more than physical stamina. It asked for emotional flexibility — the ability to switch between cities, between roles, between identities.

And somewhere along that highway, I started noticing stories.

In the back seats of shared car (car pooling), I met fellow professionals silently battling similar contradictions — chasing careers in one city while their hearts remained anchored in another. On trains, I listened to fragments of lives between phone calls, eye contact, and the occasional smile. In Mumbai's endless rush, I discovered a city that tested you before it accepted you. And in Pune, I rediscovered the value of stillness every weekend.

What intrigued me most, however, was a section of the highway that never seemed to complete — the now-famous Missing Link of the Mumbai–Pune Express way. Every commuter spoke about it. Every traffic jam on the ghat (mountain) section made you wish it was ready. Three years later, it still isn't.

And maybe that's what life feels like sometimes — unfinished projects, postponed promises, and parts of us always under construction.

That idea gave this book its name.

The Missing Link is not just about infrastructure. It's about the emotional spaces we navigate in silence — the video calls instead of dinnertime laughter, the WhatsApp photos instead of real-time moments, the "almost there"s that define modern working lives.

This book is a personal chronicle. But it's also a mirror - for anyone who has juggled work and family, made hard choices, or lived with the ache of being in two places at once.

Some journeys change your destination.

This one changed me.

The Missing Link

FOREWORD

It is a rare privilege to write the foreword for a book as intimate and truthful as ***The Missing Link***. I have known Sanjay since our earliest school days in Jammu - navigating winding childhood lanes, nurturing shared dreams, and threading our way through the alleys of expectation toward distant, grown-up cities. Life, however, had its own script. Like Sanjay, I found myself chasing dreams measured not only in air miles and office hours, but in missed birthdays and the quiet ordinariness of simply being present for those we love.

Reading Sanjay's journey stirred a physical ache of recognition, his story resonates with mine and with countless others who adapt to new environments, forge new identities, and balance professional ambition with family needs. What moved me most was his unsparing honesty about the emotional toll of commuting between worlds—the relentless Mondays, the soulful Fridays, and the bitter sweet divide of heart and place.

What has always set Sanjay apart—even in childhood—is his profound capacity for human connection. Whether befriending a guest house cook in an unfamiliar suburb, carving kinship from carpools and railway berths, or offering a listening ear to colleagues and neighbours, Sanjay's warmth makes every city less daunting, every transition less lonely. His humour and humility transform routine encounters into lifelong bonds. Many, when adrift in new cities, retreat inward; Sanjay builds bridges—with stories, with food, with empathy.

As you turn the pages of ***The Missing Link,*** you may see yourself reflected here—your aspirations, your longings, your struggles—and realize, as I did, that chasing success need not come at the cost of human connection. The truest journey is not merely from Mumbai to Pune or Jammu to London, but toward understanding and belonging, wherever life may take us.

To my dear friend and bhai Sanjay: thank you for bravely mapping the emotional highways of modern life, for showing us we are never truly alone, and for reminding us that the "missing link" we all seek is often found—imperfect but enduring—in each other.

-Sunil Koul (London)

Contents

Mumbai Dreams........ 1
Mumbai, Finally........ 5
From Dadar to Dadra (and Back Again)........ 9
The Other Side of Mumbai........ 15
Stories on the Expressway........ 20
A Bachelor, A Broker and a Bowl of Taher........ 25
The Accident........ 33
The ₹150 Cup of Dreams........ 39
Friday Nights at the Ghat........ 44
The Tunnel Episode........ 49
London Se Aaya Mera Dost........ 55
The Mumbai Monsoons........ 62
Papa, when are you back home?........ 66
The Nights and the Noise........ 71
The Night the City Spoke Back........ 75
Hooked on Malvani........ 79
The Two Extremes of Mumbai........ 83
Ganpati Bappa Morya........ 88
Closure – The Missing Link........ 92

Chapter One

Mumbai Dreams

The year was 1996.

I was in Class 10, living in Jammu - a city of calm routines, simple ambitions, and closely-knit neighborhoods. Like many students, I struggled with Hindi grammar and, so I had started taking private tuition from a neighborhood teacher. Hindi had never been my strong suit. As a Kashmiri, I had started studying Hindi relatively late. Unlike those from the Hindi heartland, the language didn't come naturally to me. While others effortlessly juggled *shuddh* grammar and idioms, I was still stumbling over *chhand* and *alankaar*.

Our tuition teacher was lean and fair, in her early 30s but not married yet. There was an air of gentle melancholy about her, but she was a kind and patient teacher. Her house - where the classes were held - was modest. The tuition room was a small one with a bed on one corner, bedding piled up in another, and a few floor mats spread out where we sat and studied. Apart from me, the class included two more boys and one girl. The teacher would always welcome me with a steel glass of water before we began class.

That day, however, the lesson was delayed.

Her brother had just returned from a trip to Mumbai - or Bombay, as we still called it - and he came in brimming with stories. A tall, slim and fit man in his mid 20s with a thin beard. He wasn't talking to me directly, but I was all ears as he sat casually on the plastic chair next to the bed, describing a world I had never imagined.

"You know, Bombay is now called Mumbai," he told his sister, with a tone of importance that made me sit up.

He went on to explain how the name had changed recently. This change was made by the Maharashtra government to honor the city's indigenous heritage and its patron goddess, Mumbadevi. I didn't understand all of it, but the sound of Mumbai struck a new chord. It sounded fresh, assertive and different.

And then he painted a picture with words.

The most modern city in India. The city that never sleeps. Roads full of black-and-yellow taxis, high-rise buildings, sea views that stretched for miles. He named places like CST, Andheri, Film City, Marine Drive, and Juhu Beach - names that floated in my head like movie titles. He said Bollywood stars walked those streets, and if you were lucky, you could spot Sachin Tendulkar himself at a signal or outside a stadium.

I was mesmerized.

In my notebook, the half-done Hindi homework remained forgotten. I was no longer in Jammu. In my mind, I was already in Mumbai - standing at Juhu Beach, eating bhel puri with one eye looking out for Amitabh Bachchan, the other scanning for Sachin Tendulkar.

That night, as I walked home from tuition through the quiet lanes of our colony, my imagination took over. I wasn't thinking about exams or school. I was dreaming - and not just dreaming generally. I was dreaming of Mumbai. It had become more than a city. It had become a feeling.

As I returned home, the comforting aroma of *Monj Haakh* - Knol Khol, a quintessential green Kashmiri vegetable filled the air. It was my favorite. My mother had prepared it with hot steamed rice and a generous bowl of curd waiting on the side. She always knows how to brighten a dull day

I couldn't wait to tell my parents the big news - "Bombay is now called Mumbai!" I blurted out at the dinner, brimming with pride as if I had just come back from a seminar with the Prime Minister.

They smiled, amused by my excitement. None of us had ever crossed Pathankot. Holidays, if any, meant trips to nearby towns or to relatives' homes. The idea of Mumbai felt almost cinematic. But even if they could not match my enthusiasm, they didn't stop me either.

Something had shifted that day.

A seed was planted - one that would quietly take root and grow over years. I didn't know how or when, but I knew one thing with certainty: Someday, I would go to Mumbai.

Not just to visit - but to live it.

And two decades later, I did — not with a camera or a tourist map, but with a laptop bag and a Monday morning deadline.

Chapter Two

Mumbai, Finally

It was a cold winter morning in November 2022.

I stepped out of my home in Pune while the city was still wrapped in fog and half-asleep. The headlights cut through the mist as I quietly reversed my car out of ground floor parking. My wife waved from the balcony, the chill in the air making her shawl flutter gently. It was one of those quiet goodbyes that didn't need words - just eyes and a nod.

This was not my first trip to Mumbai. But it was the first one that felt different.

I wasn't going there for a business meeting or a day visit. I was going there to begin a new life, at a new job, in a new company. And most importantly, I was going alone.

My house in Pune is on the eastern side of the city, and my new office in Mumbai was all the way across - on the Western Line.

That meant I would be crossing both cities completely from end to end. The symbolism wasn't lost on me. I wasn't just crossing physical boundaries; I was stepping into a new rhythm, a new routine that would become my every week.

Even though I had left on time, I stopped at the new Food Court to have quick tea and my favorite Sabudana Khichdi. The new food court was nothing like the older version I remembered from my earlier road trips. It was now a multi-storey building, developed as per a fresh, modern design. Clean, spacious, and well-lit, it looked like it was built to welcome every kind of traveller - families on road trips, corporate employees rushing to grab a bite, even solo wanderers like me.

All the big restaurant brands were now here - from global names to homegrown favourites - each jostling for attention with backlit signboards and the smell of freshly cooked snacks.

But my favourite remained the same: the old eatery that once operated out of a humble outlet on the expressway. They had now moved into this new food court and set up a neat, simple counter - but thankfully, the taste had not changed. Their *sabudana khichdi* and *poha* still had that comforting, homemade touch. I ordered my usual combo - sabudana khichdi with a steaming cup of chai - and settled into a corner.

Just ten minutes, I told myself - enough for a cup of strong chai to shake off the sleep. But Mumbai has its own rules. That ten-minute stop turned into a twenty-minute delay once I hit the city's mid-morning traffic. One wrong pause, and the city makes you pay.

As I inched through the traffic closer to my office, I noticed the shift in energy. Pune's calm was already a memory. Mumbai was alive, fast, and unapologetic. People were walking faster, honking louder, talking into two phones at once. There was ambition in the air. It felt like the city had already lived half a day before I even arrived. Mumbai's 8:30 am felt like Pune's 11 am.

But beneath that excitement, I couldn't ignore a growing unease. I was moving into something unfamiliar. The weekdays would now be spent in Mumbai, away from my family, away from the comforts of home. My son's evening stories, the warmth of my wife's tea after work, the quiet predictability of Pune evenings - all of that would now become part of the weekend only.

And not just them - my parents, too, whose silent presence in the house brought a kind of calm that only a son can feel. Their quiet support, their routines, their small questions - all would be missed in the noisy pace of Mumbai.

I reached the office a little later than expected. Nothing dramatic happened. No "first-day" celebration. I walked in, nodded at a few new faces, took the elevator, and got to work.

But something had shifted.

The boy from 1996 who had once imagined Mumbai as a city of stardust and filmstars was now navigating its realities - office entries, meeting invites, Google Maps, and weekday solitude.

There were no stars in the sky that morning.

But the city still sparkled - not with glamour, but with the grit of possibility.

And for now, that was enough to keep me going.

Chapter-Three

From Dadar to Dadra (and Back Again)

As I started settling into my new life, my solo car rides to Mumbai quickly became a thing of the past. A neighbour of mine, now a good friend, added me to a WhatsApp group for our locality in Pune. To my surprise, it had over a hundred people who, like me, commuted weekly to different parts of Mumbai.

Apparently, I was not doing anything novel. I had simply joined a silent battalion of weary warriors. And honestly, discovering there were hundreds from my area doing this same grind made the whole madness feel...slightly less mad.

Carpooling soon replaced my solitary drives. Many co-passengers turned into familiar faces, then friends, and even a few confidants over time.

In between these carpool rides, I occasionally took the train. I remember one such trip when I boarded the iconic Deccan Queen for the first time during my new job. It was a big deal for me. Deccan Queen - an iconic train, and not just for its speed or punctuality, but for the emotion it carried for so many regulars on the Pune–Mumbai route. The journey had barely started when I felt my stomach rumble. Maybe it was the early morning rush or the chill in the air, but more than anything, I was craving that one familiar thing.

Sure enough, the pantry guy came around with his tray. I ordered what many consider the unofficial signature dish of the Deccan Queen: the bread omelette. Soft white bread, slightly toasted, hugging a warm, spiced omelette - served with the kind of simplicity that only Indian trains can perfect. It wasn't fancy by any stretch, but it was comforting. It reminded me of countless other train journeys.

I took a sip of hot tea from the small paper cup and looked out the window as the city slowly faded, giving way to fields and tunnels. It wasn't just a breakfast - it was a moment that settled me into the rhythm of the journey ahead.

But that morning, the Queen betrayed me, it got delayed by 30 minutes. And in a three-hour journey, 30 minutes feels like being stuck in a WhatsApp family group you can't mute.

Sitting impatiently, watching local stations pass, I found my mind wandering - back to July 1999, when I first came to Mumbai with my father for engineering counselling.

We had travelled all the way from Jammu by train. I was not alone, many classmates from Jammu were onboard, each with their own anxious dreams packed in bags next to them. My father and I shared a compartment with a friend of mine, his elder brother, and their father.

As the train neared Mumbai, my friend's father told his elder son,

"Please enquire about a good hotel in Dadar. We will get down there and stay in a nice hotel tonight."

That line hit me. Not with jealousy, but with pure innocence, I thought he was talking about Dadra, the Union Territory near Gujarat. I had not heard of Dadar then. That's how naïve I was.

In contrast to their hotel stay, our arrangement was more... humble. We had a space reserved in a Dharmashala in the C.P. Tank area - a large hall, no individual rooms. We carried our own bedding, spread it on the floor, and somehow managed to sleep in the chaos.

This Dharmashala was a three-storey building - modest, but with a character of its own. Built entirely from large, old stone blocks, the place had an air of quiet resilience, like it had witnessed years of stories. The ground floor housed several rooms and small offices, while the first and second floors had large open halls meant for communal stay.

We were given a spot in one such hall on the first floor. From the corridor just outside, we could look down into an open area where men took baths under huge taps fixed to a stone wall - a daily ritual that somehow never looked out of place here. The sounds of splashing water, echoes of conch shells, and temple bells in the distance all merged into the strange harmony of this place.

The hall itself was massive - wide, open, and airy - lined with multiple ceiling fans that hummed above us. It was divided not by walls but by understanding; each family had carved out their own little patch of space. At least thirty families lived in that one hall that night, bustling with hopeful students like me and our parents. Each family's spot was marked by a neatly spread bedsheet, a few bags stacked in a corner, and perhaps a shawl hung from a hook.

Despite the cramped arrangement, there was a quiet sense of order. And in all that mild chaos, we never felt out of place. That crowded hall slowly became our home for the next few days - noisy, unglamorous, but undeniably human.

In that noisy hall, I found batchmates and friends. That night, we sat together, talked about our future, and laughed like we were all just on a big school picnic. There was magic in that monsoon night - I didn't want it to end.

The next day started early. Though my counselling was scheduled later, I went with my friends to their session. We reached the counselling centre early in the morning. But before that, my father and I stepped out to grab a quick bite - my first proper breakfast in Mumbai.

It was the famous Vada Pav.

I had heard so much about it - how it was Mumbai's go-to snack, quick, filling, and full of flavour. At first bite, it felt like any other Indian snack - a bun with a fried potato dumpling. But then came the magic: the dry garlic masala, and that green chilli on the side. The mix of spice and crunch, chased with a cutting chai, made it unforgettable. That was the moment the Vada Pav started to feel like Mumbai itself - simple, unpretentious, and full of character.

Fuelled by that spicy delight and the warmth of tea in our hands, we made our way toward the counselling centre, stepping into a day that would shape future of many of my friends. I of course had to wait for the next day for my turn.

The counselling centre was in one of the reputed engineering colleges of Mumbai. The campus was buzzing with nervous energy - hopeful faces, anxious parents, tired kids from long travels. I still remember how the counselling was set up in a hall adjacent to the main auditorium. It was not a sleek, air-conditioned venue with LED screens or waiting lounges.

Instead, it was a tightly packed hall, crammed with hundreds of aspirants and their families. There was barely enough space to move. People sat wherever they found a corner - on the floor, on their luggage, or simply stood. A loudspeaker placed near the stage crackled every few minutes with updates: the name of a candidate, the stream allotted, the college assigned.

In that cramped room, you could feel the weight of ambition, pressure, and sacrifice. It wasn't glamorous, but it was real - a place where many dreams would be shaped or reshaped in real time.

Most of my good friends got into prestigious colleges in Mumbai and Pune. We hugged, celebrated, and clicked mental snapshots of a life that was about to change. I realised I would not be studying with most of them again. That hurt a little.

I came back to the Dharmashala that night and tried to soak in every moment. The following day, it was my turn. I got admission in a decent college in a tier-2 city of Maharashtra. Dad and I left for Dadar station immediately to book tickets for my next chapter.

Snapped out of the memory by an announcement, I looked around. The Deccan Queen had finally reached Dadar. I rushed out, trying to get to the western line in time for my meeting.

As I elbowed through the crowd, I could not help but smile - back in 1999, I thought Dadar was Dadra, and now, it had become a routine part of my life.

The city I once feared, dreamt of, and misunderstood was now where I had to make client presentations.

Chapter Four

The Other Side of Mumbai

As I shifted to Mumbai, my company provided me with temporary accommodation in a guest house located in Mira Road, a northern suburb far from the fast-paced heart of the city. Mira Road, unlike the bustling neighbourhoods of Andheri or Colaba, had a slower pulse. It was part-Pune, part-Mumbai, quieter, more residential, and not quite the "real Mumbai" I had imagined all these years. But this is where I was to stay, at least for the first month.

The guest house was on the second floor of a nice apartment complex that had more grills than balconies, more ceiling fans than chandeliers. The living room had a decent sofa set, always covered in floral-printed sheets, a dusty television that remained on mute most of the day, and a wooden dining table with six chairs. I always took the seat closest to the balcony. From there, I could hear the traffic below, smell the vada pav from the street vendor around the corner, and catch the evening breeze that carried with it a strange comfort.

Every evening, I would sit on the same chair, sipping water from a steel glass, glancing at the news on TV. Parliament session highlights. Political debates that Mohan, our guest house caretaker and cook, had surprisingly strong opinions about.

"Sir, inka kuch nahi hone waala. Yeh sab setting hai,"

Mohan would say, half chuckling, half serious, as he served me hot rotis.

Mohan was from Darbhanga district in Bihar, a man in his early 40s with an ever-welcoming smile and a no-nonsense work ethic. He had lived in Mumbai for years, working in guest houses like these to support his family back home. He cooked, cleaned, managed the house, and somewhere along the way, also became a storyteller, philosopher, and my first real friend in Mumbai.

At first, I would laugh off his dinner invitation, telling him I was headed to Powai or Andheri. After all, this was Mumbai, the city I had dreamt of since I was a boy in Jammu, sitting in my Hindi tuition class, imagining sea views and stardust. I wanted to explore it all - the seafood joints in Andheri, the pubs in Powai, a quiet walk along Marine Drive.

But eventually, after a week of fancy food and paying extra for bottled water, I gave in and stayed in for dinner.

That night, the dining table became my favourite corner in the house.

Dal, aloo-gobhi, crisp hot rotis puffed to perfection, a small katori of dahi, and a cucumber-tomato salad with salt and lemon - all served with the same care a brother would show to a guest who mattered. The food was simple but full of warmth - and the conversation, even more so.

Over dinner, our conversations slowly turned personal. One night, when I told him that I was originally from Kashmir, his eyes lit up like a child hearing about a magical land.

"Aap Kashmir se hain, Sir?" he asked, with awe and deep curiosity.

He told me how for years he had dreamt of going on the **Shri Amarnath Yatra** in South Kashmir. He had heard stories of the track, the spiritual energy, the ***Har Har Mahadev*** chants. He also wanted to visit the Shankaracharya Temple in Srinagar and take a peaceful shikara ride on Dal lake.

"Sir, ek baar Kashmir jaana hai…….lekin haalaton ka bharosa nahi. Kashmir ke haalaat kab theek honge?" he would often ask. Stirring the dal with one hand and hope with the other.

I had no answer to that question. But I appreciated his yearning to see my homeland. There was a quiet connection between us - a man from the mountains and a man from the plains - each far from home, each carrying a piece of it inside.

Over the next few weeks, our dinner conversations became the highlight of my day. Mohan would talk fondly of his village, his kids, his annual leave. He was proud of his roots and grateful to Mumbai for giving him a livelihood. He would also begun to remember my favourite vegetables - and he would cook them with care, serving them with the smallest touches that made the food taste even better.

The man who I first saw as a caretaker slowly became a confidant.

Mira Road, which I initially thought of as the missing link between me and "real Mumbai," turned out to be a different Mumbai altogether.

One that did not shine on postcards or Instagram reels - but one that was very real, very human.

There are thousands of Mohans in Mumbai.

And maybe, thousands of people like me.

Different backgrounds, different languages, but somewhere, the same dreams - of belonging, of being seen, of building a life with meaning.

When I finally found a place to shift and told Mohan, he just smiled and said:

"Sir, kabhi kabhi dinner ke liye aa jaaiyega."

Mohan, in many ways, was the missing link in this part of my story.

Chapter Five

Stories on the Expressway

After my initial solo drives between Pune and Mumbai, a new chapter of companionship began - thanks to my neighbour Sameer, who would soon become a good friend. He added me to our area's WhatsApp group dedicated to regular Pune-Mumbai commuters. Every Monday morning, the group members would set off to Mumbai, and return on Friday evenings.

One winter weekend, I bumped into Sameer during an evening walk in our society. He was strolling with his wife. The sun had set, and there was a chill in the air. Sameer, originally from Lucknow, worked as a senior banking professional at one of India's top banks. Average built, sporting a light stubble and spectacles, he resembled Rishi Kapoor in both looks and warmth.

Sameer casually asked me about my next week's plans. I mentioned my usual Monday morning drive to Mumbai. Without hesitation, he offered, "Why don't you join our carpool? We are leaving Monday morning."

I nodded eagerly. "Sharp 5 a.m. departure," he warned, smiling. "Mumbai traffic starts early."

I assured him I would be ready on time. Come Monday, I woke up at 4:00 a.m., got dressed by 4:45, and sat with my wife for a quick cup of coffee. A little conversation, some casual exchange about the week ahead - and oops, 15 minutes had vanished without a trace.

Honestly, I don't know what hit me faster - the caffeine or the clock. One minute I was sipping coffee like a king, the next minute I was sprinting out like a courier guy who forgot the package.

I dashed to the car, only to find Sameer already seated in the driver's seat, waiting. I was five minutes late - not the best first impression. Apologizing profusely, I got in. Thankfully, Sameer smiled it off.

His car - a spacious Honda WRV - was perfect for our weekly adventures. "Two more people will be joining us," he said as we drove out of the society gate.

We soon picked up the other two gentlemen, both in their late 30s. One worked in Mumbai's music industry; the other in the insurance sector.

The three of them jumped into animated conversation as if resuming a never-ending chat. Sensing my silence, Sameer introduced me properly.

Anoop, the insurance guy, had a CEO-like presence - a smart middle-aged man with a light beard, wearing formal clothes, with the jacket of his suit draped over his arm. He had been doing this weekly commute for over six years.

Gokul, on the other hand, looked like he had stepped out of a Bollywood set — bright shirt, gelled hair, mirror-finish shoes. At 5:15 a.m., he looked like he was either going to a music video shoot or coming back from one. I wasn't sure whether to say good morning or shout "Action!"

He worked with a music label and had the flair to match.

Their talk started with who rode with whom the previous week and what return plans looked like. It drifted to their kids, school schedules, and upcoming exams.

Once we hit the expressway, the volume lowered. Everyone, except Sameer, began dozing off. Sameer, of course, had no such luxury. Lonavala approached, and Anoop suddenly piped up, "Yeh missing link ke kya news hai, kab complete ho raha?"

That was the first time I heard the term 'Missing Link.' Curious, I asked what it meant.

Gokul laughed. "Sanjay jee, aapko pata nahi? Achha, aap naye ho iss journey mein!"

He explained how the 'Missing Link' was a long-awaited expressway stretch that would drastically cut down the commute time. I felt hopeful - maybe this chaotic shuttle life would soon get easier.

The conversation died down again, and I too dozed off. Next thing I knew, we were already in Panvel.

About 45 minutes from my office, the next round of chatter began. Gokul launched into a dramatic story about Mumbai's dons, his supposed connections with influential politicians and cops, and a tale about a kidnapping that ended peacefully.

Sameer raised his eyebrows but played along, asking questions like, "Sach hai kya?"

I sat listening with growing curiosity and a bit of unease. Is this what Mumbai is like? Is life here really this intense?

Gokul didn't stop for the next 40 minutes. His monologue had all the ingredients of a crime thriller. I glanced at Anoop - he had gone silent.

Once Gokul got off, Sameer turned to me and said, "Don't take Gokul too seriously. He's a nice guy, but you will hear many such stories on these rides. Listen, laugh, and move on."

I smiled. I think Sameer sensed that I was taking it all a bit too literally.

Soon, I reached my office. As I sat down at my desk, Gokul's stories faded into the background. My to-do list took over.

But that ride marked the beginning of something new. Sameer continued to be my closest companion in these weekly rides, guiding me not just on the road but through the chaos of settling into a new city - teaching me what to take seriously, and what to just smile and let go.

Chapter Six

A Bachelor, A Broker and a Bowl of Taher

I finally moved to my new place - a rented 1BHK near my office.

But wait, it wasn't that simple. If Mumbai rentals were a game, I had just crossed Level 5 after getting slapped around in the earlier four.

I had thought technology would be my saviour. Real estate apps, filters, glossy photos, 3D views - I used everything short of a drone. But every promising listing ultimately led me to one creature: The Mumbai Broker.

These brokers are like Tinder matches - they ghost you when you are interested and flood you when you aren't. I chased brokers. They never called back. In a city with more demand than vada pav stalls, they behaved like royalty. And me? A humble commoner begging for shelter.

But the real fun began when I visited some of these flats

My expectations were shaped by Pune — where apartments are newer, more spacious, and better maintained. But in Mumbai, especially in the older pockets of the northern suburbs, buildings are typically decades old, and flats often feel congested.

Now in Mumbai, when I checked flats for rent, I found One had a bathroom smaller than the wardrobe, another had a kitchen where you could stand - but only alone. And a few had that special "Mumbai touch": a sea-facing view... if you stood on the water tank with binoculars.

Then came the society rules. No bachelors. "But I'm married!" I protested.

Society: "Are you living alone?"

Me: "Yes."

Society: "Bhaiya, bachelor ho."

I half expected them to ask for my wedding video as proof.

To make things better (read: worse), some societies had another commandment: *Thou shalt not cook non-veg*. Now, I could skip Mutton Roganjosh for a day, but living like a spinach monk? Not happening.

So when I finally found a decent, fully furnished 1BHK, it felt like winning Kaun Banega Crorepati. It was so compact that it instantly reminded me of the Munna Bhai MBBS line — "Aila, shuru hote hi khatam ho gaya!"

The society itself was nice — built on a hill, big garden, gym, swimming pool. There was even a tennis court that hosted more dandiyas than actual tennis.

But what really stood out were the cats. At least 20 of them roamed freely like they owned the place. Residents fed them morning and evening. Some even fed the stray dogs. It was like a modern-day Jungle Book, set in Kandivali.

My broker, Raju, ran his agency with his brother Mintu. Both thin, in their 30s, and bursting with confidence. Raju once told me, "Sir, ab toh koi flat shortlist karo. Aapko dikhate dikhate, humara bhi rent lag gaya."

Once I finalised the flat. The landlord used to stay in Australia.

Raju told me - "Sir, landlord wants a video interaction with you before the agreement. Just a friendly chat."

I agreed, though I found it a bit unusual. Ten minutes later, I got a WhatsApp video call from Hemant. He spoke in heavily-accented English and after a brief introduction, said, "Now my wife will speak with your wife."

Wait, what?

Why does Ruchita need to speak to his wife for a rental? I didn't like this intrusion into our personal space, but since Ruchita was sitting beside me, I let it go.

Mrs. Hemant came online. She asked Ruchita about her visits, how often she'd be in Mumbai, and so on. I sat uncomfortably, watching the conversation unfold like a bizarre matchmaking call.

Minutes after the call, Raju rang again. "Agreement can happen this week," he said. Finally, I thought - it's done.

But wait - Mumbai doesn't let you off so easily.

Raju called again next day. "Sir, just one final formality."

"What now? Blood test?"

"No sir, society committee wants to interview you."

I lost it.

"I have done a video call with the landlord. My wife has been interrogated. Now an interview with a committee? Who are these people - the Mumbai version of the CIA?"

Eventually, I agreed.

Raju reminded me the evening before, "Sharp 11 a.m., sir. If you're late, the interview gets postponed by a week."

Wow. The audacity.

On the interview day, I reached at 10:50 sharp. The treasurer, Prashant, arrived at 11:40. No apology. Just handed me his business card like he was handing a mic before a TED Talk.

He worked in QA at a top automotive firm. Suddenly, my inner salesman woke up. Potential client alert!

Half an hour later, we were deep into a discussion on the auto industry, supply chain blues and market dynamics. He ended with, "So when are you shifting? Let me know if you need help."

The society manager was so shocked, he whispered, "Prashant sir ne pehli baar kisi se itni baat ki society office mein."

And just like that, the deal was done.

I moved in.

Now, I had stayed alone in hotels before. But this was different. A hotel gives you room service. Here, I had to clean my own dishes and chase lizards.

Also, food was a problem. My area had more vegetarian stalls than humans. Non-veg was treated like contraband. Eggs? Had to walk half a kilometre.

One day over a whatsapp video call with my younger brother Sunny, I was explaining him that I feel lonely at times in Mumbai and that's when he told me that his friend Rakesh lived nearby.

Rakesh, a fellow Kashmiri, lived just a few hundred metres away. He too stayed alone, while his family was in Noida. We met the next day and instantly clicked — like friends who had always known each other.

Rakesh — polite, fair-complexioned, soft-spoken — was the Marketing Head of a major automotive company. He became an anchor in my Mumbai life.

But the shocker? He was vegetarian.

Still, food aside, we connected on everything else — work, family, loneliness.

One evening, Rakesh and I were sitting quietly on a wooden bench under the banyan tree near his society gate - a place we often ended up after long workdays. There was a cup of cutting chai in our hands and the quiet hum of Mumbai traffic in the background.

After a long silence, Rakesh said softly, *"Kab tak chalega yeh, Sanjay?"*

I looked at him, slightly puzzled. "What do you mean?"

He didn't look at me. "Yehi, staying away from family... weekdays toh theek hai, par ab toh weekends bhi chali jaati hain kabhi kabhi. All for what? For growth? For ambition? For job satisfaction?"

His words lingered in the air.

I nodded slowly. "Sometimes I feel... we end up becoming distant from the very people we are working so hard for."

Rakesh smiled faintly. "Exactly. My daughter once asked me, 'Papa, Do you work on Sundays also?' I didn't know how to answer. How do I explain to her that I'm not running away from her - I'm doing this for her"

I felt that knot in the chest again, the same one I carried every Monday morning when I left Pune.

"I know what you mean," I replied. "When I leave early on Mondays, Yavun is still asleep. I just kiss on his forehead and run away. And by the time I come back on Friday night, I feel like I have missed a whole part of his growing up. Like the week just slipped away."

Rakesh took a slow sip of his tea. "Aur sab bolte hain — enjoy Mumbai life. Kaise samjhaayein kisi ko yeh akelapan kya hota hai? The silence in a flat, the meals you eat alone, the birthdays and school events you miss…"

We both sat in silence for a moment - the unspoken bond of two fathers, two professionals, two men trying to hold their dreams and their families together in two different cities.

And then, Rakesh looked at me with a seriousness I hadn't seen before.

"Sanjay," he said, "One day, when our kids are older and they ask us about this time - I want us to have stories to tell. Not of sacrifice, but of strength. Not just about what we missed, but what we built."

I nodded. "True. And those stories... should make them proud, not sorry."

Rakesh and I met often — once, even twice a week.

One evening, he called and invited me over for dinner. I reached his place and was greeted by a lavish Kashmiri vegetarian spread — Taher (yellow rice), Dum Aloo, Tchaman Roganjosh (paneer in spicy red curry) and Lotus Stem (Nadru Yakhni).

I asked, "Rakesh, what's the occasion?"

"It's my birthday today," he smiled.

I felt bad I hadn't brought a gift. But he didn't care. We ate like brothers that night.

That night, I realised — Mumbai throws a lot at you. But it also gives back — in the form of people like Rakesh.

Meanwhile, I was fighting my daily battle with auto rickshaws. Despite living close to office, I often struggled to get a ride. Some days I walked. Other days, I offered more fare and felt like I'd won a jackpot when the driver nodded.

Amid all this — rental drama, cat society, food experiments, rickshaw haggling, and Kashmiri veg birthday parties — I began to settle down.

Mumbai hadn't made it easy. But it had started to feel like... home.

Even if the eggs still needed a trek.

Chapter Seven

The Accident

"Sometimes, it takes a crash to realize how fast we were running past what matters most."

Honestly, my job has always been dynamic - meeting new people, visiting new places, working odd hours. It helped me settle faster in Mumbai and adapt to the weekly Pune-Mumbai commute. Of course, in quiet moments, I still thought about that missing link in my life.

But life doesn't always follow the script.

In December 2023, we were in Jammu for a family wedding. And if you know anything about Kashmiri weddings, you will know they are nothing short of a week-long festival. Fun with cousins, Kashmiri music every night, the exuberant baraat, and the irresistible Kashmiri cuisine - it's the kind of chaos I live for.

By Sunday, we were flying back to Pune. Our connecting flight from Delhi got delayed, and by the time we reached home - thankfully just a short drive from Pune airport - it was night.

Exhausted, I remembered I had to leave for Mumbai the very next morning. In all the wedding excitement, I had forgotten to book my regular Monday carpool. When I checked late Sunday night, no seats were available.

So I decided to drive alone. It wasn't a big deal; I had done it plenty of times before.

But I didn't realize how tired my body truly was. A week of non-stop wedding festivities, long day of air travel, and barely a few hours of sleep that night - it was a recipe for disaster.

I left around 5 AM. Even before I hit the expressway, my eyelids felt heavy. I splashed water on my face and thought I would stop at the food court after Talegaon toll.

As I crossed Talegaon and approached the first tunnel, I dozed off. Just for a second.

And that second changed everything.

I jolted awake to find my car veering onto the divider. My hands gripped the steering wheel. I fought to regain control. It was a different world now - fear, panic, reflexes, instinct.

In that split second - as the car rattled over the divider - I don't know how, but I saw my son's face flash before my eyes. His laughter, his tiny arms around my neck. Was this it? Is this how it ends? I wasn't ready.

I somehow steered the car back onto the road, but it was barely moving. I felt a jolt through my body, but thankfully the airbags hadn't deployed - maybe the impact wasn't that strong. Still, one side of the car was completely damaged.

Drivers behind me couldn't tell - they kept honking relentlessly, impatient as ever.

With great difficulty, I nudged the car to the left side and stopped just before the first small tunnel. The front-left tyre looked dead - its outer rubber had peeled off.

It was 6 AM. Winter. Still dark. The high beams from oncoming traffic made it impossible to see. Hundreds of vehicles zipped past, their lights slicing through the fog like strobe lights in a nightmare.

I stepped out, checked the car. No fluid leaks. Just metal mangled.

My body ached, but there was no blood. No visible injuries. I ran my hands across my limbs, half expecting something to crack.

Sitting on that highway shoulder, watching vehicles blur past, I felt something unexpected - guilt. Guilt for driving when I knew I hadn't rested. Guilt for almost not making it back. Guilt for taking time for granted, as if life owed me tomorrows.

First thing I did - call the police helpline. They were quick. A towing vehicle reached me in minutes.

Meanwhile, I tried calling two friends in PCMC area, since they were staying close to the expressway. No response - silent mode, sleeping.

I thought of calling Ruchita. But I paused. She would panic. I knew her. She would rush to the accident site without a second thought. I couldn't do that to her.

The towing guy — probably in his late 20s — examined the car and said, "Aapka car ka ek side to poora chala gaya hai, tyre bhi khatam hai."

He looked at me and added, "But you are okay. That's all that matters."

He changed the tyre, helped me slowly drive 6 km to the nearest petrol pump. He then arranged a lift for me to Lonavala and suggested I get myself checked.

I sent my car to the service center in Pune. Reached Lonavala hospital. The doctor ran basic checks and assured me all was fine.

Then I caught a bus to Mumbai, sitting next to my laptop bag, still processing what had happened. My body was there, but my mind was still somewhere on that divider.

I texted my boss: "Met with a minor accident. Will be late to office."

While in the bus, I replayed the accident again and again. I realized my speed had dropped just before I dozed off - maybe it saved me.

And most of all - there was no vehicle right behind me. Had there been one, a high-speed rear collision was inevitable. I might not be writing this.

I whispered a silent thank-you to **Bhagwan Shiv** and to my **Guru Maharaj**. That day, they truly saved me.

When I reached office, I called Ruchita and told her everything. Predictably, she demanded a video call. "Let me see you," she said. I smiled and obliged.

But my heart wasn't in the office that day. I couldn't focus. I was still on that highway, swerving through the mist.

Later in the afternoon, the service center called. The repair would cost a decent sum. But for once, I wasn't bothered. I wasn't thinking about money. I was still just...grateful.

For two weeks, my car stayed in the service center - thanks to insurance delays (which many of you will relate to). I didn't drive at all during that period. I just couldn't.

But eventually, I did.

Four weeks later, I got behind the wheel again. Same car. Same seat. But a renewed respect. A strange bond. As if the car had saved me too.

And so, I drove again — not just on the road, but back into life.

There are moments in life that recalibrate everything.

For me, this accident became a reset. A gentle - yet terrifying - reminder that life doesn't give warnings. That all our plans, ambitions, appointments... they hang by a thread we often take for granted.

That day, somewhere between Talegaon and Lonavala, I lost a few seconds to sleep. But I gained a lifetime's worth of awareness.

Sometimes, it's not just about reaching Mumbai. It's about making sure we come back home.

Alive. Whole. Thankful.

Even now, every time I pass that stretch on the Expressway, I roll down the window… not to feel the wind, but to remember how close I came to silence.

Chapter Eight

The ₹150 Cup of Dreams

After I started working in Mumbai, I never spent a single weekend there. I had made a silent pledge - every weekend I shall return to Pune, no matter what. My weekends belonged to my family.

Finally, when I realised that my son had a few days off from school and my wife was dropping subtle hints like, "Tum Mumbai shift hue ho ya Mars pe?", I decided to take my family - wifey and the junior boss - to Mumbai.

We drove down from Pune on a Saturday evening. The route was obvious — our beloved Expressway. Like every ritual, we made our customary pit stop at the food court, specifically at the Sabudana Khichdi temple, which my digestive system treats like prasad. Post that spiritual experience, we took the scenic Atal Setu route from Panvel to reach South Mumbai.

I had only one plan - take them straight to Gateway of India. Not for patriotism. For Instagram. And dinner.

The crowd near Gateway was Delhi Metro at 6 PM levels. We parked the car (after doing five rounds of the block and one small prayer) and made our way to the monument.

While trying to take a "perfect family photo," we had 200 strangers in the background—a mix of photo bombers, unaware tourists, and that one guy eating bhel puri like it was a high-speed challenge.

And that's when I saw it - The Taj Mahal Hotel. Majestic. Regal. And for me, emotional.

I went into flashback mode like a Bollywood movie.

Flashback: Year 2000, Matunga Hostel Diaries

It was my second time in Mumbai. I was staying with Anmol and Rohan in their Matunga hostel. Anmol - my childhood genius friend from Jammu - was the kind of guy who did calculus for fun. Rohan, on the other hand, was the cool philosopher who knew Mumbai like a Dabbawala knows lunchboxes.

Since Anmol was busy with "microprocessor class" (or someth ing equally scary), Rohan took it upon himself to show me SoBo

Now, SoBo (South Bombay) itself is a different planet. Even their rickshaws have better English. We hopped on a local train and reached Marine Drive.

As soon as we landed, Rohan announced dramatically, "Sanjay, yeh hai Sea. Samundar hai bhai!"

It was my first time seeing the sea. For a moment, I thought it was a really big lake with commitment issues.

I stood there, wide-eyed, the breeze in my face, the salty air, the waves crashing against the rocks—it was magical. We walked on the Queen's Necklace stretch like kings without a palace, past Oberoi Hotel, where Rohan educated me on five-star ratings, high-end hotels, and whispered about how expensive everything was. Then, we strolled over to the Gateway of India, and finally stood in front of the Taj Mahal Hotel.

By the time we reached Taj Mahal Hotel, we were halfway to Goa by foot. That's when Rohan pointed at the iconic building and declared with stars in his eyes,

"Bhai, a cup of tea here costs ₹150!" he whispered, like he was sharing a top-secret defence budget.

"Someday," he said, "when we're earning, we'll come back and drink that ₹150 tea together."

And I, being the emotional sponge that I am, added it to my secret wish list right next to "learn guitar" and "get six-pack abs" - both still pending.

Back to Present: Where Dreams Brew

Now 24 years later, standing outside that very same Taj, older, wiser, and slightly better paid - I told Ruchita, "Let's go have chai at Taj.."

She looked at me like I had suggested buying a spaceship.

"Taj ke andar chai? Are you serious? Tapri wali chai tastes

better. And you get two for ₹20."

Ruchita, my ever-practical wife, never cared for luxury hotels. For her, food was about taste, not ambience. But I insisted. I told her about that old dream I had with Rohan—the two boys walking the streets of South Bombay, dreaming of affording a cup of tea at Taj someday for 150 Rs.

She melted like Amul butter. "Chalo, let's go. Let's complete your silly 'dedh-so wala chai' dream."

Inside, I was grinning like a child on a rollercoaster. We entered one of the restaurants. It was grand, luxurious, and the kind of place where even the napkins look more qualified than you.

We ordered some snacks, tea, and coffee. The bill came and guess what? The tea cost more than ₹150 now — Inflation also dreams big.

But thankfully, it wasn't alarming. It was what you would pay at any classy café. I paid happily. A sip of chai, a cup of nostalgia, and a pitcher full of memories.

And then, like a true 90s friend, I picked up my phone and called Rohan.

He answered with surprise, "Oye, bhool gaya tha mujhe?"

I said, "Bhai, guess where I'm calling from?"

When I told him I was having that ₹150 chai at Taj, he burst out laughing,

"You still remember that nonsense?! I've been to Taj a dozen times but forgot about it."

"Haan bhai, par promise toh promise hota hai," I replied.

We both laughed like the 20-year-olds we once were. Who knew tea could time travel?

Post-Chai Wanderings

We stepped out of Taj and believe me, I was more excited than my son. Like I had won a lottery that paid in memories.

We strolled through a couple of SoBo lanes and then landed at a lovely restaurant for dinner. The food was great, the mood even better.

Then back to the car and the long drive towards Kandivali — my new rented flat, my weekday home, and now, a little more special this weekend as my folks were here.

Chapter Nine

Friday Nights at the Ghat

– Where traffic moves slower than your boss replying to leave requests

Friday mornings, I am the happiest man alive - because I know by tonight, I will be back home. The thought of Pune, of home-cooked food, and sleeping in my own bed makes everything look better - even the Outlook inbox. But as the day progresses, Friday afternoons slowly morph into a nerve-racking suspense thriller.

From 3 pm onward, I start glancing at the clock every five minutes, willing it to hit 5:30 pm. But this is Mumbai, and Mumbai runs on its own set of traffic laws and Murphy's laws. A new email at 5:01 pm? A boss suddenly feeling emotionally expressive at 5:12? Or worse, a "quick call" at 5:17? That's all it takes to ruin your well-paced escape plan.

Why the panic, you ask? Because in Mumbai, a 15-minute delay in starting your journey translates to a 30-minute delay in reaching your destination. The traffic doesn't build up by the hour - it multiplies by the minute, especially on the infamous Lonavala-Khandala Ghat every Friday evening.

And that's where the real story begins...

Friday evenings now seemed like a marathon. When you run a 42.2k marathon, you pace your run based on elevation, weather, water stations, and the target finish time. Similarly, when we - me and my carpooling gang, many of whom are good friends now - start our journey from the Western Express Highway in Mumbai, we pace ourselves for the journey ahead.

It always began on the Western Express Highway. Like a mini war council, everyone in the car would open Google Maps simultaneously and then began the debate of the century: "Which route today, gentlemen?"

JVLR? Santacruz-Chembur Link Road? BKC? Or the newest temptation—Atal Setu. Of course, Atal Setu would be vetoed by the economist in the group because of the ₹250 extra toll. There was one guy in the group – Parag - who would check petrol prices by district before approving a route. Legend says he once saved ₹7 by detouring through Uran.

Over time, I started believing that no matter which route we took, we would reach Vashi at the same time anyway. But the discussion was mandatory. A ritual. A stress reliever. A comedy show. Everyone had an opinion, none of it ever made a difference.

Once we crossed Vashi and hit the expressway, the real test of character began. And by character, I mean patience. Because waiting for us like an old frenemy was the Lonavala-Khandala Ghat traffic jam. If sales targets were tough, this was tougher.

As soon as we crossed Khalapur Toll Naka, a synchronized chorus would begin: "Check Google Maps! Check the ghat! What's the delay today?" No one was asking if there was traffic. The question was: "How long is the red line today?"

Three kilometers of bumper-to-bumper? Normal. Five? Acceptable. But if you saw double digits in delay time, someone would inevitably go, "Bas karo yaar, yeh toh Mahabharat chal raha hai." The WhatsApp group would start buzzing with memes and complaints.

Every time, as we crawled near the Amrutanjan Bridge, someone would groan, "Yeh Missing Link kab complete hoga yaar?" And another one would add, "Har kisi ki life mein ek Missing Link hota hai, Sanjay. Tabhi toh life interesting banti hai."

But one Friday, something unexpected happened. We saw a convoy of cars with flashing red-blue sirens - clearly VIP movement. The collective reaction in the car: Ab toh gaya kaam se, ye toh pure highway ko bandh karwa denge.

But surprise - the convoy took a turn before the ghat. Sameer, my ever-enthusiastic carpool buddy, jumped with excitement: "Bhai, follow kar isko! VIP log shortcut le rahe hain, hum bhi lenge!"

The driver of the day, Gautam, obeyed like a rally driver. We swerved behind the convoy like amateur Fast & Furious extras and found ourselves on the old Mumbai-Pune highway.

There was a bit of traffic police around, but none stopped us. Within no time, we were in Lonavala, bypassing the jam entirely, and back on the expressway ahead of the jam.

Someone screamed: "Miracle! Miracle!" and Gautam cranked up the volume. Just then, as if FM radio was our personal DJ, the song playing was "Aaj main upar, aasman neeche". We laughed so hard, we almost missed the turn.

Of course, good times don't last. Next Friday, the road was one-way and guarded by cops. But now we were hooked. If there were no cops, we took the shortcut. If there were cops, we practiced the ancient art of acceptance.

Eventually, we stopped cribbing. The ghat jam became a space for reflection, deep talks, bad jokes, and worse singing. From career ambitions to random Bollywood trivia, nothing was off-limits.

But no matter how serious or silly the conversation, one thing remained constant- Hanuman Ji ka darshan. Every car, every Friday, every time – we bowed our heads near the little Hanuman temple just before Amrutanjan Bridge. It became our weekly ritual. A spiritual pitstop amidst chaos.

And just like that, our Friday marathons became less about frustration and more about friendship, funny routes, food stopovers, and faith in the middle of the madness.

They say life is a journey, not a destination. But on Friday evenings, life was the destination - and that destination was Pune. Over time, our carpool became more than just a ride - it became a support group, a debate panel, a comedy club, and sometimes even a spiritual retreat (especially when we prayed for traffic to move).

We cursed the traffic, mocked the system, chased VIP convoys, and treated Google Maps like an unreliable old friend - but we always reached. Eventually. And in those long hours of crawling through the Ghat, we discovered something deeper: that perhaps the real 'missing link' wasn't just a road on the map. It was the part of life that teaches you patience, the value of conversations, and how laughter can make even a traffic jam feel like a joyride.

So the next time you're stuck bumper to bumper, maybe don't just honk—look around. Your next story might be sitting right next to you.

Chapter Ten

The Tunnel Episode

It was one of those rare weekends when I didn't rush back to Pune on a Friday evening. Shocking, I know. But this time, I had a good reason, I was meeting my old colleagues for a long-overdue breakfast in Vashi on Saturday. And trust me, this plan had been rescheduled more times than an Indian monsoon.

The breakfast was everything I hoped for - hot idlis, piping sambhar, and the timeless tradition of bashing bosses. After parting ways, I boarded my afternoon train from Thane to Pune. A comfortable 2A side lower berth, perfect weather, and a full belly-what more does a man need for a nap?

Within 15 minutes of boarding, I was in deep sleep - snoring probably louder than the engine.

Next thing I remember was being jolted awake by the sweet voice of an angel yelling, "Vada Pav, Vada Pav!" Karjat station. I opened one eye, checked my surroundings, confirmed my location, and slipped back into semi-snooze mode.

The train started again. I remember passing Palasdhari, a small station with a name that sounds like a peaceful hill resort but is actually just a sleepy stop. Somewhere between that and Lonavala, I must have dozed off again.

And then… everything changed.

When I opened my eyes next, I was still in my berth—but something was off. The coach was lit from inside, but outside? Pitch black. Not dim. Black. Like someone had painted the windows with Vantablack.

I pulled out my phone instinctively. No network.

Refreshed. No network.

Moved to the door. No network.

Checked others' faces. Everyone had the same expression: confused, semi-sleepy, and borderline concerned.

One group of four young boys—still buzzing from their sugar and soda overdose—were chatting at the door. I asked them what happened.

"Sir, train tunnel mein hai. Shayed signal problem."

"How long?"

"10 minutes... I think."

Ten became twenty. Then thirty. Then forty.

And I wasn't sleepy anymore. I was restless. Not the "stuck-in-Lonavala-traffic" kind of restless. This was different.

I wasn't just stuck in a train. I was cut off from the world.

No signal. No idea where I was. No idea when we'd move. Just the metal coach creaking slightly every few minutes, dim yellow lights, and outside—a suffocating, oppressive darkness.

I looked out and realised we were on a curve. The tunnel bent ahead like a black python, coiling further into the unknown. For a moment, I wondered—what if we never get out? Yes, drama queen alert, but in that moment, it felt real.

I spoke to some fellow passengers—many elderly folks—who were now wide awake and growing anxious. I tried to calm them, all the while calming myself. "Kuch nahi hoga, signal issue hai bas," I said with a fake confidence that would've made even a politician proud.

But inside, I was rattled. This was not a traffic jam on the expressway. This was isolation. The kind that makes you realise how dependent you are on your mobile phone. On connectivity. On knowing where you are. On feeling seen.

We had disappeared into a black hole. No one could reach us, and we couldn't reach anyone.

It was supposed to be a three-hour journey. But one hour into that, I felt like I was floating in some intergalactic limbo—with a bunch of strangers, echoing silence, and zero network bars.

I even thought: If this train doesn't move soon, I'm walking out of this tunnel—even if I have to crawl.

Some younger folks were already debating if walking ahead

with phone torches was a good idea. I didn't stop them. I might've followed too.

And then... just when our patience and oxygen were running out... the train jerked slightly.

Movement.

From the coach behind us, someone clapped.

From my coach, someone actually muttered, "Thank God."

And in that moment, as the wheels began to roll, I felt like we were survivors of a zombie apocalypse. When we emerged into the daylight near Khandala, it wasn't just a geographical transition—it was emotional. Like being reborn after a near-death experience involving old tunnels and no Jio coverage.

The four boys—still energized—broke into impromptu applause. I wanted to hug them. But then again, boundaries.

By the time we reached Lonavala, my phone lit up like Diwali. Dozens of missed calls. I called my parents. Then, of course, I called Ruchita.

Her first words: "Where were you? What were you doing? Tumhara phone kyu off tha?"

I tried explaining.

"You were stuck in a tunnel? For one hour? Kya Titanic mein the?"

I narrated the whole episode to her, hoping for sympathy. I got sarcasm. Marriage, ladies and gentlemen.

Later that evening, I did what any traumatised millennial would do: Googled the number of tunnels between Karjat and Khandala. Turns out—there are 28. Yes, twenty-eight tunnels. Built in the 1860s. By the British. Angrez chale gaye, tunnels chhod gaye.

And now, every time I travel that route by train, the moment we pass Karjat or Khandala, my eyes stay wide open. I keep track of tunnel number one… two… five… ten…

I'm not afraid of the dark. I'm afraid of being stuck in a place where the world doesn't know you exist.

And maybe, just maybe, someone who enjoys solitude, who finds peace in silence and pitch-black nothingness, would've loved that hour of stillness. But for me? The always-on, chatty, connected-to-20-WhatsApp-groups extrovert? That was nothing short of psychological waterboarding.

So yeah—after that day, tunnels aren't just tunnels to me. They're a reminder of what it feels like to be truly disconnected. Not metaphorically. Literally.

And honestly? I will take expressway traffic over tunnel silence, any day.

Chapter Eleven

London Se Aaya Mera Dost

While Mumbai may not boast about the weather of Pune or Bengaluru, or the wide, glassy roads of Delhi, the city stands apart - not just for being India's financial capital, but for being the home of Bollywood, one of the country's most developed cities, and, above all, a place stitched together from the fabric of people's dreams.

Mumbai holds a special place in the minds of those from Tier-2 cities. Whenever I tell someone in Jammu or Srinagar that I work here, the first question often is -

"Mumbai mein kahan rehte ho?" And when I say 'Kandivali', many of them are like – 'yeh Mumbai mai hai kya?' as if Mumbai starts with Andheri and ends at Bandra.

Some old uncles back home ask, "Bachchan Sahab ka ghar kitne door hai tumhare ghar se?"- as if Amitabh Bachchan were my neighbour and we exchange Sunday brunch invitations. Others ask, "How far is the sea from your place?" I am used to it now.

The upside is that over the last three years, many friends and relatives have had reasons to visit me in Mumbai - some for Mumbai darshan, some on work trips, and some just in transit before an international flight. And I enjoy every bit of it because I love being with people - especially my own people.

The Return of a Childhood Friend

One of the most memorable visits was from my childhood friend you have already met - Anmol, the studious guy from Chapter 8. After engineering, Anmol went on to do his PG in business from one of India's top B-schools. And as they say in Hindi - "Banda ban gaya woh."

Today, Anmol works in London, having lived in some of the world's greatest cities. One day, completely out of the blue, I got a text:

"Bhai, coming Monday to Mumbai."

I was overjoyed as if I had just heard that India had become the number one economy in the world. "Come, bro, waiting for you!"

He landed close to midnight after a nine-hour Heathrow–Mumbai flight. Mumbai's T2 arrival terminal at that hour is a scene in itself. The glass façade glowed under the soft yellow lights, the giant lotus-shaped ceiling shimmering above the long rows of arriving passengers. Outside, the exit gates, there were chauffeurs holding placards, and family members craning their necks every time the automatic doors slid open.

And there I was, standing with my hands in my pockets, feeling oddly like a Bollywood hero waiting for the climax reunion scene.

When Anmol finally appeared with his trolley bag, wearing a travel jacket and that familiar half-smile, it was like no time had passed at all.

We didn't need words, just stepped forward and hugged immediately.

That brotherly warmth, the kind that doesn't fade with time or distance, flooded in.

It was the same joy we had felt as kids in the lanes of Srinagar and later in Jammu, when the biggest problem in life was whose turn it was to bat first in cricket.

We walked towards the parking area, and I said, "Let's grab a coffee at Starbucks before we head home. It's just around the corner."

He stopped in his tracks. "Bhai... London se aaya hoon. Heathrow pe teen Starbucks dekhe hain... ek to boarding gate ke samne hi tha. Tum mujhe Starbucks le jaoge?"

I grinned. "So?"

"So??" He widened his eyes. "Mumbai aaye hain... aur tum Cutting Chai ke badle mujhe cappuccino pilaoge? Tum to wahi aadmi nikle jo Goa jaake vegetarian khata hai."

We both burst out laughing. Of course, we ditched Starbucks and went to a tapri just outside the airport complex. Two paper cups, steam rising in the humid night, the clink of steel spoons in glasses, it felt perfect.

After chai, we drove to my flat in Kandivali.

Now Anmol, having stayed in places like Singapore, London, and Dubai, was used to apartments with Alexa-controlled lighting and automatic blinds. So when he walked into my cozy 1BHK rented flat, he looked around and smiled politely, "Nice… very compact."

I laughed. "Say it clearly, bhai - 'Aila, shuru hote hi khatam ho gaya!'"

He noticed that my living room was also the dining room, study, and possibly a guest bedroom. Before he could judge more, I handed him the remote: "Netflix is the same in Mumbai and London. Pick a show and pretend you are in Soho."

The next morning, he was greeted by the typical Mumbai morning medley - temple bells, kids crying, uncles discussing politics, and cats meowing like they were the landlords.

We stepped onto the balcony with our tea mugs. He saw the cats being lovingly fed. "Yeh sab teri society ke hain?" "Haan, 20+ cats and 100+ humans. Perfect balance of power."

He also noticed the gym and tennis court. I added, "The gym is mainly decorative. And the tennis court is for Diwali Melas."

Being with Anmol again was like stepping back into the lanes of Srinagar or Jammu when we were kids, running around, sharing stories, and dreaming about the future. From those small-town streets to our college days, we had roamed together then, and now here we were, roaming around Mumbai.

That afternoon, we went on a nostalgic trip to his engineering college in Matunga. We stopped our cab well before college and decided to walk, passing by what locals call '5G' - Matunga's five famous gardens. (Trust Mumbai to have 5G gardens before mobile networks.)

Anmol said, "Bhai, yeh mere student days ka Cuffe Parade tha."

We entered his college, strolled through the corridors, and, of course, went straight to his old canteen.

The canteen uncle looked exactly the same—just with a little more white in his hair and a little more 'inflation' in the price list. We ordered omelette pav, and as soon as it arrived, Anmol held it like a sacred relic.

"Bhai, same taste. Sirf bread aur ande ka size chhota ho gaya hai. Aur bill ka size bada."

We laughed, took a few photos, and in that moment, it was as if the years had melted away. We went out looking for a chai ke tapri, to have Anmol's favourite Cutting again.

Somewhere between sips of chai, the friendly India–England rivalry kicked in.

Anmol: "London traffic is bad, but yeh Mumbai ka traffic… bas, Olympic-level patience ka test hai."

Me: "At least here you can get out of the cab and buy vada pav at a signal. Try doing that on Tower Bridge."

Anmol: "Weather though… London ka weather classy hai."

Me: "Classy? It rains every 15 minutes there. London ka mausam toh mood-swing ka chacha hai. Mumbai at least warns you in monsoon - 'Bhai, agle teen mahine bheegna padega.'"

We both ended up laughing so hard that the chaiwala thought we might not pay the bill.

As much as the trip was about nostalgia, there was also an undercurrent of something deeper. Anmol's life today mirrors mine in an unexpected way.

He works in London, but his family lives in Singapore. When he moved from Singapore to London for work, he couldn't move his family immediately. So, like me, he lives alone during the week, visiting his family every 2–3 months.

That evening, over dinner and a couple of drinks, we talked about it. How chasing professional dreams - dreams that are important and fulfilling - often means putting parts of our personal lives on hold. We spoke about the small moments we miss, especially watching our kids grow.

And, as has been the tradition whenever we drink together, we played our favourite Jagjit Singh ghazals. No evening is complete for us without *Thukrao ab ke pyar karo*. As those hauntingly beautiful notes filled the air, the conversation slowed. The glasses clinked, the words grew fewer, and for a moment, the music said everything we couldn't.

There was no resolution - because there is no easy resolution. We just acknowledged the truth of it. The conflict sat there between us, like an uninvited guest neither of us could ask to leave.

The next morning, we were back to our old selves - teasing, laughing, planning where to eat next. But somewhere inside, I knew this visit wasn't just about nostalgia. It was about realising that no matter where life takes us -London, Singapore, Mumbai, there will always be some things we chase, and some things we miss.

And maybe that's the deal life offers: you can't have it all, but you can choose the people you share it with. In my case, if that comes with a cup of cutting chai, an omelette pav, and Jagjit Singh in the background - well, I will take it.

Chapter Twelve

The Mumbai Monsoons

Having lived in Pune for a large part of my life, monsoons always held a special place in my personal calendar. In Pune, the rains arrive like a cool blessing after months of dry heat. Within weeks, the surroundings transform - Lonavala, Khandala, Mahabaleshwar, Tamhini Ghat, everything turns lush, green, and postcard-worthy.

Monsoons in Pune are romantic, refreshing, and if you ask a true Punekar - essential for survival. Because here is the thing: Pune depends heavily on rainwater for its year-round water supply. The dams around the city store the rainwater, and if the rains are delayed or weak, water shortages become very real. So, like every Punekar, I would eagerly await the monsoon's arrival. It wasn't just weather, it's an annual exam we hope nature grades us well on.

When I began my weekly Mumbai commute, I knew the monsoons here would be different. After all, who hasn't heard of Mumbai's legendary rains - the ones that can turn the financial capital into a giant swimming pool? I still remember the July 2005 floods - trains stalled, people wading through waist-deep water, office workers returning home looking like they had swum the Arabian Sea. We had heard and seen it on almost all news channels.

Naturally, I was curious and a little apprehensive. I hoped to experience the rains without experiencing the havoc. My first real taste came while driving from Pune to Mumbai that monsoon. Near Lonavala, the downpour was so fierce I could barely see the road. Wipers at full speed, headlights on, speedometer crawling at 10 km/h and still, visibility was like trying to watch a cricket match through frosted glass.

But that was the expressway - famous for its weather mood swings. The real Mumbai monsoon introduction came one weekday morning.

It had been raining heavily for two straight days. The weather apps were flashing red alerts, schools were declaring holidays, and Twitter was flooded with pictures of... well, floods. My office was nearby, but even getting an auto was a challenge. After multiple rejections (and a couple of drivers who looked at me like I had just asked them to drop me to Baramulla), I finally found one willing to go.

The auto dropped me about 100 metres from my office gate, not because he didn't know the way, but because the road ahead looked more like the Yamuna in full flow. I opened my umbrella, which instantly revealed itself as a purely decorative item. Rain came from the top, from the sides, possibly even from underneath. By the time I stepped inside the office, my shoes were making that *chap chap* sound usually reserved for bathroom slippers, and my socks were so wet they could have been donated to the Fisheries Department.

I thought, Well, that's it. Surely half the office will be empty today. After all, I lived close by and still struggled. Many colleagues lived 40–50 km away. To my shock, almost everyone was already there - early, dry, and working as if the weather outside was just a rumour.

When I asked one colleague how he managed, he said casually, "We are used to it. In monsoon, we always carry a spare set of clothes. No big deal. We have seen worse." Another laughed, "Real Mumbai monsoon starts the day local trains stop. Till then, it is just a warm-up match."

That day, I understood what "The Spirit of Mumbai" really means. It is not just a slogan – it is people showing up, rain or shine, without excuses, without drama, and in some cases, without even in dry clothes.

From that moment, I stopped cribbing and started enjoying the rain.

From then on, Mumbai monsoons became part of my weekly story. But there's one aspect I could never fully adapt to - landing in Mumbai during monsoon.

See, my work involves lots of travel and a significant part of it is air travel. And Mumbai monsoons mean thick clouds - the kind that look like they have been stitched together just to hide the city from pilots. Approaching Mumbai, you often feel like the plane has entered a grey eternity. You keep waiting for that moment when the clouds part to reveal the city… but instead you just keep diving deeper into more clouds, wondering if Mumbai has quietly relocated while you were away.

And then there is the turbulence - that delightful "free fall" sensation mid-descent. The coffee trembles, your seatbelt digs into your waist, and you suddenly remember every unpaid bill in your life. On the ground, I had adapted, learned to carry an extra shirt, wear rain-friendly shoes, and walk into the office like I had just returned from a spa instead of a swim. But in the air? Every landing felt like a lottery ticket.

Over time, even that became routine. That is the Mumbai way - it tests you, then trains you to survive it.

If Pune monsoons are poetry, Mumbai monsoons are prose - urgent, relentless, and unapologetic. They drench you, delay you, and sometimes scare you. But they also teach you resilience, patience, and the art of laughing when your socks are wet.

Chapter Thirteen

Papa, when are you back home?

Outside my Mumbai office window, the city was in full evening chaos, honking cars, impatient bikers trying to squeeze into impossible gaps, and the occasional street vendor yelling louder than the traffic itself.

Inside, the chaos was different - a dozen voices on my work call, all talking over each other like they were auditioning for Indian Idol.

And then… my phone buzzed.

Video call from home. My son.

In that moment, the noise outside, the noise inside, everything faded.

I muted my call immediately - not because I am bold, but because… priorities.

Before I could even say hello, he fired the question that always melts me:

"Papa, when are you back home?"

It's such a simple question, but it hits harder than any sales target.

In that moment, I mentally opened my *Papa–Visit Calendar*. The sad truth? It was starting to look like the Mumbai–Pune train timetable - full of delays, cancellations, and "subject to weather conditions."

I smiled and said, "Bas beta, aa raha hoon Friday ko.."

He nodded, but then came the killer line:

"Okay, but don't get your laptop this time."

Ouch. That one stung.

Because he was right - even when I was home, half of me was still in Mumbai, working at times or on a call. Physically present, mentally in Excel.

That is when I realised the "missing link" here wasn't just the distance between Mumbai and Pune - it was being present while being there.

In our house, my visits had become a mix of a festival and a cricket series.

My son marked "Papa arrival" days in his diary with giant smiley faces.

My wife, ever the planner, would "book" me for family events the way you book a marriage hall - months in advance, with reminders.

Sometimes, even my parents in Pune would ask, “Beta, is baar kitne din ke liye aayega?” as if I was an NRI visiting from Toronto, not from 160 km away.

Before Mumbai happened, evenings were mine - helping my son with homework, having chai with my wife, and those random ice cream runs to our favourite Natural ice-cream parlour after dinner.

Now, those moments had turned into “special occasions,” and special occasions had become… rare.

Earlier, my son’s daily question was, “Papa, dinner mein kya hai?”

Now it was, “Papa, dinner kab karenge… saath mein?”

Weekends in Pune had their own template:

Friday night: Reach home late, looking like a refugee from the Mumbai traffic war.

Saturday: Family breakfast, catch up with errands, maybe a social event, maybe a movie if lucky. Maybe a drink with my dear friends in the evening.

Sunday evening: Already packing to leave, pretending I am not leaving.

Honestly, I now spent more time packing and unpacking my bag than actually enjoying what was inside it.

Leaving Mumbai on Friday evenings (or Monday mornings in reverse) had its own rhythm - traffic jams near Chedda Nagar flyover, the sigh of relief after clearing Panvel, the green embrace of Lonavala Ghat, and finally that emotional shift when you see the first familiar signboard of Pune.

But while the drive reconnected me physically, the real connection - the real missing link - happened only when my son ran to hug me, shouting "Papa is here!"

One weekend, over dinner, my wife and I spoke about how this routine was affecting family time.

We both knew the job was important - it was part of the dream we had worked for. But staying away from home, was also costing us moments that don't come back.

My son, quietly listening, suddenly said:

"Papa, kaam important hai… lekin aap bhi important ho."

Game. Set. Match. Ten-year-old wins the life lesson championship.

That day, I thought about all the Mumbaikars I had met - the resilience, the way they show up for work in rain, floods, or traffic jams.

That's the famous Spirit of Mumbai.

But for me, the spirit I needed most was the one that made me show up - truly show up - for my family.

I promised myself small but meaningful changes - keeping my phone aside during family meals, blocking calendar slots for school events, and saying "no" to calls on certain weekends.

Targets and deadlines will always be there.

But my son's Sunday morning football match? That's non-negotiable.

After all, in my son's world, the real missing link is just Papa being there - no laptop, no calls, just me.

Chapter Fourteen

The Nights and the Noise

That weekend in Pune, after my son's "Papa, when are you home?" moment, I felt more aware than ever of how precious our family time was.

But come Monday morning, the emotional warmth had to make way for Mumbai's high-speed rhythm. The city had its own pull - buzzing meetings, endless deadlines, the mad energy of office banter, and the colleagues who were fast becoming friends.

And while Pune gave me the comfort of belonging, Mumbai gave me the thrill of momentum.

It was in one of those weeks, fresh from a sales high and still riding the wave, that we decided to celebrate. A midweek party - because why should Fridays have all the fun?

So that week on Wednesday evening, we decided to go out to celebrate our last month's sales success. Everyone was in high spirits. We wrapped up work early, changed into casual clothes, and headed to a pub in BKC to toast a milestone in our business growth story.

BKC was buzzing that night. Mumbai pubs have their own charm - they don't judge you on your looks, your clothes, or whether your hairline is still where it used to be. They are the flag bearers of diversity and inclusion. Walk in wearing a blazer, a T-shirt, or a "just got off a local train" look - the welcome is the same.

Inside, the pub was alive with music, laughter, and the clink of glasses. I noticed a lot of young people - clearly students - enjoying themselves like it was the last night before a major exam (and I suspected some of them might have had one the next morning).

For a moment, I wondered how these kids could afford such upmarket places. Then I reminded myself - this was 2024, not my college days. The world had changed. Why on earth was I still comparing everything to my days?

In my college days, I studied Mechanical Engineering in a Tier-2 city — a department where spotting a girl was as rare as finding an apple tree growing in Mumbai. Even talking to a girl was a big deal, forget going out for a cup of chai.

But I was always... different. A little stubborn when it came to challenges. I had friends across departments — many of them girls from Computers and E&TC. And, true to my "aim high, miss often" personality, I'd somehow only end up falling for girls who were already dating someone else. Maybe it was the thrill, maybe it was bad luck, but it was definitely a different world.

Now, in this BKC pub, I looked around at a generation for whom sitting with friends of all genders over drinks was just… normal. A part of me felt happy for them, another part felt slightly jealous, and a third part reminded me to finish my drink before the ice melted.

Somewhere between our second and third round, one of my colleagues — famous in our team for turning into a complete nautanki after just two pegs — started his usual act.

"Sanjay bro… 10 pegs down, still standing da machi!" he declared dramatically, as if he had already completed some sort of Olympic feat.

The thing was — he had only ever handled two pegs in his entire drinking career. So naturally, the rest of us took this as a personal challenge.

"Chalo, da machi… aaj Olympic final hai," someone teased.

Before he knew it, we had actually made him drink 10 pegs. By the end, he was on the dance floor with us, pulling moves that would have made Govinda reconsider his own career. The next day, he had absolutely no idea what had happened — possibly the first time in his life he'd gone beyond two pegs. We told him he was outstanding… though in reality, he was barely standing.

The music was loud enough to make conversations louder. One colleague was passionately explaining Bitcoin despite having no investments in it, another was negotiating "just one more plate of fries" with the waiter like it was a business deal.

We laughed, clicked photos, and promised to do this "every month" — promises that would evaporate the moment the next sales target hit the table.

By 11:30 pm, the night began to fade. I was in a cab heading back to Kandivali. The city's noise faded into the low hum of the engine.

I unlocked my apartment and stepped into silence. Just hours ago, I'd been surrounded by people, energy, and noise. Now it was just me, my bag, and the fridge humming in the corner.

The irony was sharp — I wasn't lonely in Mumbai. I had friends, dinners, laughter. But the belonging was still 150 km away in Pune. Back home, the night would end with my son's hug and my wife asking, "Kuch khana hai?" Here, it ended with reheating leftovers and scrolling through photos from the evening.

Before sleeping, I sent a quick voice note to my son:

"Beta, sorry, we could not do VC tonight."

Within a minute, the two blue ticks appeared, followed by his reply:

"Papa, see you on Friday"

And just like that, even after the fun, the music, the dancing, and the "10 pegs down da machi" moment — I felt that quiet, persistent missing link._

Chapter Fifteen

The Night the City Spoke Back

It was a Thursday night, and I returned from another team dinner in Mumbai.

Same routine — shoes off, keys on the table, fridge door open for cold water.

Usually, this was the part where silence walked in before I could even lock the door.

But that night, before the quiet could settle in, there was a knock.

I opened it to see the couple next door — a Bengali couple in their early 40s, who used to stay in flat next to me.

We had exchanged polite smiles in the lift a few times, the "Haan, weather acha hai" type conversations that never went beyond the 6th-floor button.

The husband was the HR head at a big banking company, his wife worked with an IT firm in Goregaon.

Between their work schedules, it seemed like they spent more time inside the lift than inside their own flat.

"Bhai, we are having a small get-together at our place. Aaja, khana khake jaa," the HR head said.

I hesitated for all of two seconds. The alternative was another night staring at my phone screen, scrolling through Instagram reels of 90s Bollywood songs and travel influencers.

So I went.

Their living room looked like someone had taken all of Mumbai's diversity and put it on one sofa set.

There was a retired Parsi couple, a graphic designer from Shillong, an HR manager from Indore, a struggling actor from UP, and a couple who ran a tiffin service.

Food was everywhere - Momos from the corner shop, Maggi cooked in bulk, and one mystery dish everyone swore was delicious but no one could name.

At one point, my Bengali neighbours decided the evening needed music.

The husband pulled out his phone, connected to a tiny Bluetooth speaker, and before I knew it, we were singing old Bengali songs together - him with full emotion, me fumbling through the words but catching the tune.

Apparently, in their dictionary, being invited meant being expected to sing.

The struggling actor clapped along, the Parsi uncle tried to join in but mixed the lyrics with Gujarati, and the whole room dissolved into laughter.

One neighbour insisted, "Mumbai mein survive karna hai toh do cheezein hamesha stock rakh - Maggi aur whisky."

The retired uncle added, "Aur patience. Woh toh free mein aata hai traffic ke saath."

The struggling actor shared that his flat was so tiny, "guest bedroom ka kaam kitchen karta hai... and sometimes bathroom too."

He wasn't from our society but a friend of theirs, living in a nearby society. Tall, lean, with sharp eyes that carried both hunger and hope, he introduced himself as an aspiring actor. He had come to Mumbai three years ago with nothing more than a small bag, and a dream bigger than the skyline.

Over dinner, he began sharing his story.

"Mumbai is brutal," he said, between bites of biryani. "But Mumbai also gives you hope every morning. Har din lagta hai, aaj kuchh hoga. And that's enough to keep going."

He spoke of sleeping in cramped shared rooms with six others, of waiting endlessly outside casting offices, of being rejected more times than he could count. "But rejection bhi ek school hai," he smiled. "It teaches you patience, thick skin, and jugaad."

I was struck by his resilience. For him, the city wasn't just about survival - it was about belief.

"Yahaan har light post ek stage hai, har local train ek acting class hai," he joked, making everyone laugh.

And in that laughter, I realised — this was another version of the spirit of Mumbai. My missing link was family, his was opportunity. But both of us were learning the same lesson - Mumbai tests you, pushes you, but it never lets you stop dreaming.

When I left, the corridor smelled of rain-soaked concrete and someone's freshly brewed chai.

Distant horns hummed in the background, mixed with the faint echo of laughter from that living room.

For the first time in a long time, walking into my flat didn't feel like walking into a vacuum.

The missing link was still there - my family was still in Pune, my weekdays were still here - but for that night, the gap felt smaller.

On the couch, I thought maybe the missing link is not always about people from your past.

Sometimes, it's about letting new people in - the ones who make your Thursdays feel less like Thursdays.

Chapter Sixteen

Hooked on Malvani

Mumbai is a melting pot of people, languages, and — most importantly for a foodie like me — cuisines. Over time, I had already tasted everything from Italian pizzas to Lebanese shawarmas, from Burmese food to Thai currys.

But it was one evening with a colleague that rewrote my Mumbai food story.

One of my colleagues, a proud son of the Konkan coast, declared after work one day,

"You haven't lived in Mumbai until you've had proper Malvani food."

The way he said it, I felt like I had been committing a crime all this time by not tasting it.

That night, he dragged me to a small but bustling restaurant. The air there wasn't just filled with the aroma of food, it was a full-on spice parade marching straight into my nostrils. I could smell coconut, fresh fish, and a red masala so bold it could probably get a seat in the Parliament.

The menu was a new world for me — Kombdi Vade, Mutton Malvani Masala, Bombil Fry, Surmai Curry. My colleague ordered for us like a seasoned general planning an ambush.

As we waited for the food, my colleague leaned forward.

"Bro, Malvani spice is not like your mild butter chicken in Pune… this is the real deal. You ready?"

I smirked. "I'm from a hostel mess, yaar. We've eaten stuff that could dissolve a steel plate. Bring it on."

He laughed, "Let's see if you're still talking after the vade hit your stomach."

One bite into that Mutton Malvani Masala, and I realised this was not food, the is was an emotion, with chilli. The fiery red masala was unapologetic, the coconut milk was soothing like a peacemaker, and the kokum added that tangy twist, like a friend who cracks a sarcastic joke in the middle of a fight.

I had eaten spicy food before, being a Kashmiri, growing up in a Tier-2 city, hostel mess food had sometimes been so spicy that it could strip paint off a wall. But Malvani spice was different — it didn't just burn your tongue, it took your soul on a Konkan road trip and brought it back smiling.

From that day, Malvani food became my weekly ritual. Wednesdays often meant rewarding myself with a seafood dinner, some weekdays sometimes called for a lazy lunch with mutton masala and vade. I quickly mapped out at least three or four Malvani haunts - each with its own charm. A homely joint for "comfort food after a tough week," a mid-range family restaurant for when friends dropped in, and a posh outlet for those days when the craving hit but the expense account was footing the bill.

My very first solkadhi experience is still etched in my memory. I had no idea what it was, a pinkish pink drink served in a steel tumbler. I thought it was some strawberry milkshake's shy cousin. I took a big gulp expecting sweetness... and my taste buds went into emergency mode.

It was tangy, salty, spicy, coconut-y - all at once. My eyes widened, my colleague laughed so hard he nearly choked on his vade.

"Arre, this is solkadhi, not falooda, Sanjay!" he said.

Ten minutes later, I loved it. That's the magic of Malvani food — it shocks you first, then hugs you forever.

One Friday, just before heading home, I had a sudden idea — why not take Malvani food for my family in Pune? I packed a feast: kombdi vade, bombil fry, mutton masala, and of course, the now-beloved solkadhi.

When I reached home, I proudly opened the packets like I was unveiling a new invention. My wife took one look and said,

"This smells... intense."

My son poked the bombil fry suspiciously, as if it might still be alive. My parents were more diplomatic - they politely took a few bites, smiled, and then quietly reached for the pickle and rice as "backup."

By the end of the meal, my son had decided that solkadhi was "pink soup for grown-ups," my mother declared the mutton "too spicy for dinner," and my father said,

"Beta, nice... but next time bring misal pav."

That night, as I sat finishing the leftovers alone, I smiled. Maybe they didn't get Malvani food the way I did. But for me, it wasn't just about the taste — it was about bringing a piece of my Mumbai life back home.

And in that moment, between spicy mutton and soft vade, I realised - sometimes food is not just food. Sometimes it's your way of closing the gap between two worlds.

Chapter Seventeen

The Two Extremes of Mumbai

Mumbai has everything - from the glassy skyscrapers that scrape the clouds to the sprawling slums that hug the city's belly. And what makes it unique is how often you will find them standing right next to each other, co-existing like reluctant roommates. Over time, I realised it wasn't just geography, it was survival. Each depended on the other in strange, invisible ways.

One evening, I was reminded of this contrast in the most dramatic fashion.

An industrialist I had recently met and known, called me. A man I knew as tough-as-nails in business but charming outside work, he casually said,

"Kal dinner ke liye aa jao. Small get-together Rakha hai."

I did not think twice. I am always excited about such invitations, who wouldn't be? The next evening, I drove to his home in

Bandra, expecting maybe a large bungalow. What I found instead was a four-storey mansion.

The moment I stepped in, I felt I had landed on the sets of *Hum Aapke Hain Koun*. Twin staircases sweeping up like wings, chandeliers throwing light like waterfalls, and a décor that whispered both royalty and cinema.

The gathering was surreal. Familiar Bollywood faces mingled with business tycoons. Well-known singers set up a mehfil and started performing. Imagine sipping your drink while listening to hit songs being sung live, right next to you. Heaven didn't feel so far away that night.

The drinks were names I had never even heard of, let alone tasted. Starters ranged from delicate chicken kebabs to seafood that felt like it had been flown straight from the ocean to my plate. After a few glasses and many songs, I texted my wife on WhatsApp:

"We are behind the world… the gap with some humans is so much that it will be really difficult to compete with them, at least in this birth."

Her reply came back instantly, in her usual grounded way:

"We are good, very good. We have whatever we want in life."

I just sent her a "hmm." But her words lingered with me.

This evening remained etched in my memory. Honestly, such moments only encourage you to do better professionally and I had the same feeling that night.

A Few Months Later

One morning, months after that Bandra mehfil, reality knocked in a different way.

I woke up and realised I had a conference to attend, but my suit - jacket and trousers, were not ironed. It was just 7 a.m. I rushed downstairs and asked the security guard if there was any laundry or pressing shop open.

He pointed me towards a small lane, "Sir, abhi ek hi dukaan khula hoga. Idhar se seedha chaliye."

I walked down 400–500 metres and suddenly found myself in a slum. I had never imagined such a settlement existed so close to many posh societies around.

The lanes narrowed as I walked further. Water flowed on the streets - some from utensils being washed, some from kids bathing outside their homes. Cleanliness was clearly a luxury here. For a moment, I felt I had entered a different world, miles away from the Mumbai I knew.

And yet, even here, amid all this, a small temple stood tall. People thronged there, offering prayers. I paused, folded my hands, and paid obeisance to the Almighty.

Finally, I found the laundry shop - a middle-aged man in an undershirt and shorts pressing clothes. I hurriedly requested him to iron my suit. At first, he said, "Time lagega, sir." But seeing my urgency, he smiled and added, "Ab aap itna bol rahe ho… to kar deta hoon."

As he ironed my suit, I looked around. Many homes lacked toilets, children ran barefoot, and life looked fragile. I instinctively texted my wife:

"We should thank Mahadev for whatever he has given us in life."

Her reply came in seconds:

"Is that you, or has your phone been stolen?"

Later, when I returned to my society, I told the guard, "I got my suit pressed… but it was deep inside the slum."

He just shrugged and said matter-of-factly:

"Sir, apne society ke sab maid wahin se aate hain."

That's when it hit me - the dependence. The slum dwellers powering the lives of the mansion residents, the invisible chain keeping Mumbai moving.

Mumbai is not just about me walking from a mansion to a slum in two different weeks. This contrast plays out for millions, every single day.

A maid who cleans a sea-facing duplex in Bandra, only to return home to a one-room-kitchen in Dharavi.

A banker who spends the day handling million-dollar deals in Nariman Point, then squeezes into a crowded Virar fast local at night.

A driver who drops his boss at the airport for a business-class flight, and then lines up for ration rice on his way home.

This is the real Mumbai - not just a city of extremes, but a city where these extremes depend on each other. The mansion cannot function without the maid. The corporate office cannot run without the security guard. The gated society cannot operate without the electrician from the chawl nearby.

And somewhere in the middle are people like me, the so-called "middle class professionals." We oscillate between air-conditioned boardrooms and waterlogged roads, between pubs in BKC and iron shops tucked inside slums. We too are part of this giant balancing act.

If you look closely, every Mumbaikar carries their own "missing link." For some, it's money. For others, it's time. For many, it is simply dignity. But what keeps this city alive is not that everyone has found their missing link - it's that despite the gap, they continue to move forward. To hustle. To survive.

That is the real paradox of Mumbai. The two extremes may look worlds apart, but in reality, they are two sides of the same coin. And maybe that's why the city never sleeps - because it cannot afford to.

Chapter Eighteen

GANPATI BAPPA MORYA

Ganesh Utsav, the ten-day celebration, has always held a special place in my heart. In Pune, these days weren't just about rituals - they were about joy, togetherness, and tradition woven into the fabric of the city. No matter where you came from, once you lived in Pune, Ganesh Utsav became yours too.

Our society celebrations were vibrant, but the highlight for me and my wife was always our annual "darshan yatra" to the five ***Manache Ganpati*** – starting with Shri Kasba Ganpati. We would step out late at night when the lights, decorations, and energy transformed the city into something magical. The peth areas came alive, not just with prayers but with the very soul of Pune.

So when I moved to Mumbai, it was natural that I missed this deeply. Festivals are not just events, they are markers of belonging. And in the beginning, Mumbai didn't feel like home.

Discovering Mumbai's Ganesh Utsav

One afternoon, during a casual lunch, I overheard my colleagues talking about the big pandals in Mumbai. Out of sheer excitement, I jumped into the conversation and by nightfall, I had made up my mind: I would explore them myself.

That night, I took a local to Currey Road station and walked towards Lalbaugcha Raja. The moment I stepped out, I felt I had entered another world. Lanes bursting with people, lights, food stalls, police trying to manage the crowd, and the unmistakable vibe of devotion. The air was thick with chants of "Ganpati Bappa Morya".

But my colleague's words rang true - the crowds were massive, and darshan wasn't easy. I moved on to Ganesh Galli and then to Chinchpokli Cha Raja, Parel Cha Raja, and many others. Each pandal was a spectacle - the themes, the grandeur, the sheer devotion on display. And everywhere I looked, there were youngsters recording reels, declaring proudly, "Guys, we are at Lalbaugcha Raja!" I smiled to myself - Instagram would surely be flooded that night.

Even businesses were not left behind. From FMCG giants to industrial brands, banners and hoardings lined the streets, all seeking Bappa's blessings for growth. After all, Ganpati isn't just about endings; he is about auspicious beginnings.

As mesmerizing as it was, Mumbai's Ganesh Utsav felt different from Pune's. The scale here was larger, the pandals more extravagant, and the crowds endless. But what I missed dearly was Pune's weather. In Pune, even after hours of walking through pandals, I never felt exhausted. Here in Mumbai, after a few hours, the humidity wore me down, and I found myself sitting at a bus stop, catching my breath.

And another missing link hit me - in Pune, Ganpati visits were always with my wife and friends. Here, I was alone. The grandeur couldn't hide that absence.

As I returned home late that night, tired but content, I realised something profound. Both Pune and Mumbai celebrate Ganesh Utsav differently - but in both, the heart of the festival is the same: faith, hope, and community.

The missing link for me wasn't Bappa. He was everywhere. The missing link was company - the familiar faces, the shared laughter, the collective awe.

Still, I went to bed with a smile. Because in both cities, one truth remains unchanged: during those ten days, life pauses, struggles fade, and Bappa makes everything feel possible again.

Ganpati Bappa Morya!

CLOSURE – THE MISSING LINK

Life, I have realised, is not about having everything perfectly connected. It's about learning to live with the gaps, the delays, the detours, and still finding joy in the journey.

For me, The Missing Link began as just a road project on the Mumbai–Pune Expressway, that frustrating patch that delayed my weekend reunions with family. But as I travelled week after week, and lived through accidents, friendships, colleagues, festivals, monsoons, pubs, food, tunnels, and traffic jams, I understood something deeper:

We all have our own "missing links."

Sometimes it is distance from family.

Sometimes it is time we don't get back.

Sometimes it is dreams we keep chasing while life quietly happens in the background.

And yet, these missing links don't weaken the story of our lives. They make it richer. They add pauses, emotions, humour, and even pain, but also give us lessons, resilience, and stories worth telling.

If you have read through my journey, I hope you found glimpses of your own life between these pages. Maybe in a late-night commute, in a drenched umbrella walk, in a child's innocent question, or in the laughter of colleagues over 10 pegs.

For me, writing this book has been about joining the dots between work and family, between Pune and Mumbai, between what I had and what I missed.

And the biggest truth is this: the missing link never truly disappears, it becomes the bridge you build with your own choices, love, and hope.

So, the next time life feels incomplete, don't just search for what's missing. Look at what it's teaching you. Maybe, like me, you'll discover that the missing link was never a gap, it was the reason you kept moving forward.

Until the next journey.

Onwards. Always.